Gudrun Heller

Side by side
...with Bob Dylan

AF192073

Poems as a tribute to Bob Dylan at his 75th birthday

© 2016 Gudrun Heller
All rights reserved.

Production and publisher:
BoD – Books on Demand, Norderstedt

ISBN 978-3-844-81492-7

Annotation

In 2015, I published the book of poems „Seite an Seite...mit Bob Dylan" as an e-book in Germany.

As a tribute to Bob Dylan on the occasion of his 75th birthday, I now translated the poems in English, added some new ones and published them as paperback version.

Hope you´ll enjoy them!

Preface

Sounds and words are like waves. They touch each other and carry forward for all eternity. Sometimes, a sound touches a sound, sometimes a word and sometimes the other way round. We, who are swamped with them, somewhen can hardly recognize what has been there at first, and who has touched whom.

I only know for sure, that in the stream of Bob Dylan´s words and music, the following poems emerged.

Contents

Poems about Bob Dylan

Poems inspired by
Bob Dylan´s songs

On the way

Heavy boots beat on the asphalt of the street
which once you had built on your own,
with the blood of your heart
and your soul´s confidence,
and many dreams you have forlorn.

Now you´ve been on this road for ages
and dust whirls around your feet,
it´s been a long time
since you´ve found here something,
and even longer
that there was someone to meet.

So many senseless marches,
so many efforts to sustain,
meanwhile you lost the sight of your goal,
and it seems like you have lived in vain.

Man from the north

If you are travelling
far up to the north,
where the winds hit heavy
against the dike,
remember me of one
who lives there,
he is the only one
I ever loved with might.

If you are travelling
far up to the north
at a time
where the storms are raging,
see for me, if he´s still alright,
and if the sun still chases
his awful night.

If you are travelling
far up to the north,
see for me,
if his dark eyes still glow,
if the desire still burns in them
as it did as he stood on the dike of the sea.

If he still wears his shirt half open
and the blackness of his hair
still breaks the blue heaven,
because this is the beautiful image
I saw when I fell in love with that man.

And sometimes I do suddenly feel
as if he just had to think of me, too,
my heart begins to jump for joy
by the thought that his love
could have once been true.

So if you are travelling
far up to the north
where the winds hit heavy
against the dike,
I beg you to take my light with you,
maybe it brings my love back to him
with irresistible might.

The street musician

At the corner of our village square,
there stands a street musician,
he collects the coins in his cap,
while looking for oblivion.

He sings from longing and from loving,
from luck in a far-off country,
I stand in front of him to listen
to this unexpected bounty.

To never lived out feelings
his music leads me softly,
and I feel like I could finish the things
that in the past, I´ve quitted mostly.

His songs are giving wings to me,
together, we are floating to nowhere,
and easiness firmly seizes my soul,
makes it shine like scarcely before.

We are charging through the biggest waves
and the wind blows through our hair,
climbing laughingly on top of the dunes –
and suddenly you are there.

I had almost forgotten you,
buried you in the deepest ground,
now you have risen from the dead,
but I forbid you to make any sound.

Instead I make my way back home,
as fast as I can do,
my wings I have certainly lost and forlorn,
they are still lying on the shore.

Fare thee well

Stand up, my friend,
you got to go now,
our past is gone
and there´s no future anyhow.

My road lies in the shadows
and yours is illuminated by a bright light
there is no bridge to be seen between them
and to me, this seems to be right.

For you, it was never important
to understand what I was feeling,
and your world was strange to me,
now it´s time for a quick leaving.

I don´t regret anything,
and I don´t mourn after you,
in the night, the street led me here,
now it takes me away,
without any clue.

If this is love I don´t know by now,
feelings always go their own way,
no one has the might to change them
or to force them to stay.

So stand up, my friend,
you got to go now,
I don´t give you a goodby,
just fare thee well somehow.

Give me an answer to it

Why do I have to shout at you,
though I can understand you well,
why does luck have to vanish so fast,
crumbling away to hell?

Why do have people to kill other people,
when living is much more beautiful,
why do the other ones have to starve,
and you´re becoming too fat,
even against your will?

Give me an answer to it,
before my heart bleeds out,
give me an answer to it,
if you don´t want me to shout,
give me an answer to it,
before it gets too late,
give me an answer to it,
before everybody has to hate.

Why do the children have to cry
and nobody is there to console,
why is mercy so very rare,
why do all these people turn away?

Why do you pass the beggar by,
who urgently needs your help,
why do your ears remain so closed,
why does your soul refuse to yelp?

Give me an answer to it,
before my heart bleeds out,
give me an answer to it,
if you don´t want me to shout,
give me an answer to it,
before it gets too late,
give me an answer to it,
before everybody has to hate.

How long do I have to tell you about it,
though you can hear everything by yourself,
how long do I have to point my finger at it,
before you can see without my help?

How long do we have to search for solutions,
when a handshake works the problem out,
how can worldwide hatred ever end,
when even you can´t love
and are filled up with doubt?

21

You can´t give me an answer to it,
not you and me either, my friend.
Cause the answer is buried in the river of life,
in which everything is united in the end.

Over stones with strange signs on it,
its water flows since forever,
under some of them lie the truth telling words
that give an anwer to all this ever.

But you won´t find the river
as long as you are living,
because its words can only be understood
if you´re dead and God is willing.

The gliding flight

Your soul rose up to the sky
a long, long time ago,
success had made it so light
that it could easily fly.
Higher and higher up to the stars
it seems to be bound to win,
and meanwhile it surely has forgotten
how easily one falls down from the sun.

Its summer seems to be never-ending
and it is living in abundance,
while it watches other souls rising,
but never believes
that they´re having a real chance.

But somewhen, there will come the time,
in which only others can fly really high,
and in black letters the end of its fame
is written into the sky.

Gliding down from the highest heights
back down to the low valley,
back down to where we all must live,
there is left no other alley.

But if only for a moment, it had been clever,
it suspected the end of its luck and glamour,
and safekept in its heart for worse times
a big piece of its summer.

Nothing and nobody

You were flying so very high,
everyone cheered on you,
and at every place where you appeared,
nothing but people, all fans of you.

You thought they all were loving you,
and would walk together with you,
now you´re standing on your own,
and no one is interested
in what you do.

You have never understood,
that it is no good
to sport with other one´s feelings,
all the broken-hearted women
are playing with you,
just for their own healing.

You can call out as loud as you can,
but they will never turn around,
they will only see through you and
just remain silent.

And slowly,
you finally understand,
it was not you whom they were loving.
It was the glory and the fame
to which they were eagerly shoving.

Now you are standing here on the street,
and nobody even knows you,
you have no idea of how to earn money
and just for your name,
you won´t get anything to do.

Take your children by the hand at last,
they have been waiting for you so long,
take a look at your wife´s face,
before she refuses to keep crying on.

And finally you will understand
that you are on the very bottom,
you are a nothing and a nobody,
bound to be forgotten.

Plan of fortune

You want to have someone by your side
who takes the load off you,
someone who patiently runs the house
with which you don´t want to have anything to do.

Someone who rears the children
always on her own,
never ever grumbling a bit
about being so often left alone.

Someone with whom
you can have much fun,
if you are once back again,
someone to be shown on a party,
which promotes your career then.

But this is not my plan of fortune,
my dream of life runs a different way,
I´m not only your fortune´s adjunct,
you can´t force me here to stay.

To make career on the cost of others,
that´s really not my business at all,
daily duties are surely no pleasure,
but I don´t play the deaf when they call.

Either both of us become lucky
or you go your way on your own.
Maybe you will find another woman
who likes to be the shadow of your sun.

You have to decide now
what´s more important,
I´m already sitting on a packed case,
I´m not willing to wait any longer,
you have to judge if I am to chase.

Give my freedom back to me

Beautiful pictures of you everywhere,
how can I really forget you?
Beautiful pictures of you everywhere,
tell me what am I to do.

You say
it is not your fault,
that I fell in love so crazily,
you say
it has never been your aim
to let me suffer so heavily.

Goddamn player,
you know exactly what I mean,
goddamn player,
your lies will be unmasked soon.

Give my freedom back to me,
you do not love me anyway,
give my freedom back to me,
from you, I have to turn away.

On the lighthouse

Off the coast
there is a lighthouse
since ages and ages ago,
the guard is retired for a long time,
but the ships still come and go.

When everything goes over my head
and nothing will bring relief to me
I climb up right onto its top
and listen to the songs,
that are sung
by the wind of the sea.

It tells a story of foreign countries
and people who believed in life as pure fun,
and I admit I was one of them,
all day long playing in the sun.

But that life is not all guns and roses,
me and you know only too well,
therefore don´t let us waste our time,
afar already glows the red evening sky.

So we both sit on top of the lighthouse
regarding the ships come and go.
They are passing by
like my life,
always in danger of sinking
or moving too slow.

The goodby

You are living so nearby heaven,
in dizzy, icy height,
here, mistakes are only made once,
nature is anxious to defeat.

Your family lives all crushed together
in this little hut,
your father is in charge of you,
if he speaks
all mouthes have to be shut.

Give me a kiss to take along,
give me a kiss before I go,
give me a kiss to make me believe
that you love me though.

Everything
that you have learnt here,
you needed to survive,
reading and writing is unknown to you,
shelves full of books
never belonged to your life.

Bound to the earth is your life,
and so your love is, too,
if I now leave I will feel no pain,
and it´s the same for you.

Give me a kiss to take along,
give me a kiss before I go,
give me a kiss to make me believe
that you love me though.

Yet, you don´t really love anybody,
your faith is sworn to the stars above,
there´s only little feeling left for me,
I can´t call that love.

But your tenderness is overwhelming
and goes beyond any limit,
here, where only nature counts
and nobody thinks of money
as worth struggling for it.

At the end of the street

What remains at the end of the street?
What remains at the end of the day?
What will finally persist
from all these years on the way?

A handful of memories,
a handful of luck,
a lot of wrong tracks,
much laborious back.

Will I have finally met you
at the end of the avenue?
Or will I lastly yet become happy
without ever having touched you?

Anyway,
your image will chase me
until the end of time
because this love is too big
that I can ever forget its shine.

Not much is needed
to stick forever in one´s memory,
and sometimes a short moment is enough
to create eternity.

Today is our day

It´s been such a long time
since you went away,
it´s been such a long time
since we saw us every day.

And now you´re standing
at my door,
it takes time till I can believe it,
and I´m so very gay.

No matter how long you are staying,
no matter how long you´ve been apart,
everything what counts to me now,
are the next hours close to your heart.

How much tears did I cry,
how many letters
did I send to you?
But the more letters I did send,
the more came back to me.

Today,
we take our hearts in our hands,
climb up to the highest mountain,
and fly back again.

You dance with me
till late in the night
and everything
that has been obscure and dark
will become clear and bright.

Today the earth
can´t keep us at the ground,
today we laugh at gravity,
no one can keep us from strolling along,
everything´s light and free.

Today the guns are singing
and the cats are barking,
horses are squeaking
and the birds are stalking.
Today there are no depths,
but only bridges,
and poor soldiers turn
into rich men with crutches.

And the reason for all this,
let me say:
All this happens
because it´s our day!

Forever wild

For your long journey
I wish you good luck,
don´t let yourselve be retained
and don´t stay back.

Rely on your compass,
you feel inside,
it shows you the direction,
when fog misguides.

Your heart shall stay
forever wild,
untameable strong
and curious like a child.

Try out everything
which seems to be worth trying
and listen to the ones
you can rely on.

Friendship and love may stay with you
for the rest of your whole life,
they are the ones that finally count,
without them it´s hard to survive.

Your heart shall stay
forever wild,
untameable strong
and curious like a child.

Your head shall never be too soft
and your heart shan´t be too rough,
I wish you much of true awareness,
paired with love and kindness enough.

And don´t wait for the end of the street
to find your fortune at last,
your luck is lying beneath your feet
and is easy overlooked,
if you´re running too fast.

Day of freedom

Now it´s been such a long time
that you´ve been caged up here,
in darkness and deep desperation,
no chance to escape from there.

What has been yesterday,
you have forgotten,
and tomorrow is out of reach,
the others say you are not guilty,
but you can hear the lie
flaring up in their speech.

What was wrong and what was right,
none of both really matters here,
only the hunger for freedom counts,
and the greed for the sun
in this darkness severe.

And a song is sung
by the wind in the trees,
and sent out as far as to the moon,
it´s singing of your day of freedom
that surely will tear up your chains soon.

You no longer need anybody
to protect you and prevent you from falling,
you have already found your way,
you only have to start rolling.

Black shadows

Black shadows are settling down on my soul
robbing the light of the day,
demons are rising up to the air,
destroying all things
that are precious for me.

Once again
living at the end of the world,
once again
eclipse of the sun,
once again
there´s no air left for breathing,
once again
no getaway route to run.

Fighting against the well-known black powers,
I cloister my soul away from you,
beating on everything that comes nearer,
being nothing more than a howling animal
scratching at your door.

And for a long time
I´m no longer in this world,
leaving back only the shell of my body,
everything of my soul is now shattered,
turning into something ugly and moody.

Once again
living at the end of the world,
once again
eclipse of the sun,
once again
there´s no air left for breathing,
once again
no getaway route to run.

Jajo

I see their feet
close beside yours,
your feet are in big,
theirs in little shoes.

Jajo, oh Jajo,
why does fate forces me
to destroy great luck?
Jajo, oh Jajo,
why am I destined
for not being loved back?

She is a beauty
with long, blond hairs,
she gives you the power
you need during the years.

Jajo, oh Jajo,
I can´t give you anything,
that you don´t call your own,
Jajo, oh Jajo,
send me to hell,
steal my crown.

But I know since long
that this won´t happen,
so I force myself to go
and take fast action.

Jajo, oh Jajo,
why is it so hard
to destroy a dream?
Jajo, oh Jajo,
how long do I have to listen
to my heart´s scream?

The train from the mountains

Sometimes light falls on those
who always stand in the shadows,
and suddenly you are frozen in shock
about the crowd which we leave behind
beyond the green meadows.

There are little
who earn more and more
and more and more
who call little their own,
it really tears my heart into pieces
and makes my face deeply frown.

Be careful, my friend,
there´s a train in the mountains,
winding down to the valley.
Who is overrun by its mighty wheels,
dies slowly on its long alley.

It´s enough to raise a child on your own
or to be older than 50 years,
and already you are sorted out,
damned to poverty and to tears.

Why should I be
still interested
in the problems of the world,
when directly in front of my door,
everything is sold out?

Be careful, my friend,
there´s a train in the mountains,
winding down to the valley.
Who is overrun by its mighty wheels,
dies slowly on its long alley.

Further and further on

There is something deep inside of me
that I have to pursue,
further and further and further on
until I reach the last clue.

It flows through my vains
and rushes through my head,
it makes my heart dance,
shows me the next step.

I got no choice,
got to go away from here,
I can´t tell you whereto,
only far from thee.

I shake the dust
off my feet
and put them on the way,
I am bound
to be running fast,
at least until the next day.

There were many people in the past
who wanted to keep me straight in the line,
but I am bound to go further and further,
keep on walking until I´ll feel fine.

The second me

It´s been a long time
since a strange longing
took hold of my soul.
It no longer was content with the possible,
only the impossible had to be its goal.

And should the impossible
be obtainable
even against all odds,
it would rapidly take to its heels
and betake itself into the woods.

Apparently today is one of the days
I see the second me in my mirror,
apparently today is one of the days
self-deception won´t distract me
from seeing my own true horror.

And I hear the two
quietly swearing
deep inside of me,
no one will ever survive to see our true nature,
that´s what we guarantee.

In my bed now lies a strange man,
whom I desired since so long
because of his beauty and his charm,
now all of this seems to be wrong.

I get up and run
further and further
only away from him,
and the further I run
the lighter gets my soul
leading me back to my former goal.

Apparently today is one of the days
I see the second me in my mirror,
apparently today is one of the days
self-deception won´t distract me
from seeing my own true horror.

And I hear the two
quietly swearing
deep inside of me,
no one will ever survive to see our true nature,
that´s what we guarantee.

I am so fed up with not being able
to finally arrive at my aim,
and I hate this curious longing
that never ceases to burn.

The fog deeply falls
down on my soul
and I can´t understand you no more.
It´s unlikely that you ever did,
so it´s better to walk out of the door.

Apparently today is one of the days
on which everything looks like rain,
so everything old is thrown away
and the eternal wheel spins all over again.

The other world

What the hell are you doing here,
a renowned celebrity
among ordinary people
or for you, what are we?

Do you really believe
you are one of us,
still feeling and thinking
in the patterns of must?

Your time among us
has long gone by,
and I tell you
no one really wants you to stay.

Even if they argue in another way,
you will never be like us no more,
and the rumour of your visit
has reached us long before.

People are talking jealously,
but not into your wide open ear,
even so that doesn´t matter
because you´re not willing to hear.

You are still under the illusion
that we are all friends of you,
it would be better for you to wake up at last,
for your world is far away from here.

You have decided to leave us behind,
and now there is no way back.
It´s a fact that the two worlds are hardly bridgeable,
but nobody will tell you that.

Rely on yourself

Don´t think that I would help you
in your struggle to find the right way,
as if my life was full of signposts
made just for you to see.

Only you yourself
can give the right answer,
there´s no one who can do this for you,
you know by yourself
which way is the right one
and what is false and what is true.

You have always been on your own
in this hostile world,
no one ever takes responsibility for your faults,
except when he is paid.

And don´t think my feelings
for you are love,
don´t be so very romantic,
you´re just another object of my lust
which I enjoy
till I got enough.

It´s time for you to start to learn
just to rely on yourself,
you will see it soon won´t matter
what others think and if they help.

Born in another country

The words pale on the horrible gate
of the time of execution,
the tracks still lie as a reminder
and will hopefully do
until the end of evolution.

And no one will ever touch my soul,
in the way that man of America did,
nothing can ever lead me out of the dark
like his music does
every time I´m unable to talk.

Full of hatred was the time
and you could smell the blood in the wind,
of millions and millions of Jewish people
who were killed and buried and left no hint.

Now they are trying to forget
what never can be forgotten.
But we need the knowledge of the past to learn,
or else our future will be shot down.

And no one will ever touch my soul,
in the way that man of America did,
nothing can ever lead me out of the dark
like his music does
every time I´m unable to talk.

If he had lived here in these years,
he would have surely died, too,
as one of the millions
who were sent into the gas
or killed by the death squads
which everywhere flew.

Full of ideas and full of talent,
has there been someone like him
also among us?
I dread to think of all these people,
of all these lives wasted thus.

And my soul would have been poor,
without this music written by him,
thank God he was far away from the evil,
born in another country
with another kind of men.

What good am I for?

What good am I for,
if I can´t even dry your tears
and you have to hold me tight
to disperse my horrible fears?

If the floor wavers
beneath my feet yet
and I´m unpredictable
in which direction
I make my next step?

What good am I for,
if I´m so far away
from all the others and their world,
if I can hardly build a bridge to them
which will not be destroyed?

What am I fighting this battle for,
which I have already lost a long time ago,
a fight for truth and a better life,
for dignity for me and you?

What is all this misery for,
if nothing changes in the end,
what is all this life´s struggle for,
when by death life is finally bent?

Tight connected

I run through the streets
seeking you,
but my search is completely in vain,
I guess I´ve been away
too far and too long,
it looks like I can´t gain.

Nevertheless, I don´t fear
not to see you again,
deep inside of me
I know this can´t happen
cause your heart is too much
bound to mine.

And then I suddenly detect a man,
quite accurate kind of your style,
and I can hardly realize the wonder
that I found you just passing by.

We can´t help
but laugh at each other,
so happy to see love at work,
and there´s still the same magic between us,
we don´t have to talk.

And we both will never fear
that we won´t see us again,
cause our hearts
are too tight connected
right up unto the end.

Brown eyes

At the end of a long summer´s day
it draws me out on the streets again,
I take a seat in the cafe
right opposite to my cosy home.

I want to see the coloured chaplet
of various blossoms one more time
and how the green leaves are blowing
in the summer wind so fine.

But it is like bewitched,
and I can´t believe my eyes,
because today everything shimmers
in your brown-eyed ways.

The street musician at the corner
sings a song of this world´s sorrow,
of cruely dashed and forlorn love,
and money´s power over tomorrow.

But I´m afraid he got no chance,
his words can´t reach me in any way,
because today I can´t believe my ears,
for everything sounds brown-eyed today.

A friend sits down near beside me
with questions I ought to answer,
I look at her face and I don´t know
wherefrom I should take the words
to content her.

Because today,
I can´t believe my tongue,
it merely refuses to talk,
no matter how much I try to speak,
everything becomes
a brown-eyed dialog.

And slowly I begin to understand
I live in another world,
nothing seems to matter much,
but only your brown eyes count.

Otherwhiles not

Mostly,
I have everything under control,
mostly,
I can hide my tears fairly well.

Mostly,
I can see my way clearly in front of me,
mostly,
I know exactly how my future has to be.

Mostly,
I can contain myself,
even when you´re spreading
rumours about me,
I can manage to keep quite calm
and finally laugh about thee.

Mostly,
I can hardly remember
any feelings for you.
Mostly,
I can´t really believe I once thought
I had found a love so true.

The burden on my shoulders
grows heavier from year to year,
I am used to carry it alone,
that´s not what I fear.

Everything is mostly and otherwhiles not,
and I´m not sure
which is more important
and which I ought to forget.

The stranger

There was neither a farewell
nor a letter,
and he was searching in vain for something
that could explain him the matter.

The door was wide open
but his luck had been gone,
as a remembrance on the table,
a glass half-full of water
was to be seen.

They said she met him
on the outskirts of town,
they spoke strange words,
that nobody had ever known.

And she committed her heart
to the hands of this man,
to the hands of the stranger
of a far off land.

She never wondered
whether it was right or wrong,
she just had to follow him down,
her feelings were too strong.

Sometimes your luck has to wander,
and you don´t know for which reason,
but only if you let it free,
it can return in another season.

Where has dignity gone to?

People barrow in dustbins
in search of waste glass and food,
you yourself have tossed something in there
that you haven´t eaten up.

Tell me, where has dignity gone to,
please, show me the way to find it.
Tell me, where has dignity gone to,
release me from the desperation
I have to cope with.

People are walking down the streets
with everything they own in a plastic bag,
they have lost all of their hopes
for human kindness to get.

And when the night
falls down on the city,
no one cares any more,
and love is bought
because it´s lost
and no one shows any pity.

Tell me, where has dignity gone to,
please, show me the way to find it.
Tell me, where has dignity gone to,
release me from the desperation
I have to cope with.

At the slot machine in the gambling casino,
there sits an old and lonesome man,
he does nothing but to play in his life
and no one knows since when.

Tell me, where has dignity gone to,
please, show me the way to find it.
Tell me, where has dignity gone to,
release me from the desperation
I have to cope with.

Fed up with your love

You say that you love me
and I should be happy of this,
but my mirror shows dark under-eye circles
of a heart that is stuck in the mist.

I see you walking down the street
and I wish you would never come back.
I see you walking down the street,
give way to another luck!

I´m so fed up with your love,
why do you still feed me?
I´m so fed up with your love,
it´s time to release you.

Your heartbreaking words
are without a true feeling,
I have since long read your face,
I know you act double-dealing.

Underneath your bright exterior
I see your true face at last,
I don´t know why I should love you any longer,
so I have to break up fast.

I´m so fed up with your love,
why do you still feed me?
I´m so fed up with your love,
it´s time to release you.

Sunset

I am sitting here in the sunset
and first shadows fall down on the light,
it is not yet dark,
but with the night, the day begins to fight.

My feet are tired from the long way
that led me away from there
and I start asking myself,
what was it that brought me here?

I can still feel them,
hatred and love,
feel the scars on my soul,
that the pain made tough.

Meanwhile it´s been already
such a long time ago
that I travelled around,
such a long time
that I hardly remember
what was the reason to go there
and was there anything to be found?

I´m no longer seeking happiness
in the other ones eyes,
because luck is always followed by pain
and I don´t want the pain to rise.

I read your letter,
it is truly nice,
but soon I have forgotten the words
though they sound quite wise.

Yet I can´t see
why I should keep them in mind,
anyway, I´m too old for you,
and it doesn´t matter in the end
that they are really kind.

There are no exciting news
that you can tell me about the world
because I have heared all of its lies
and I have seen the blood in which you stood,
ready to give death and to die.

Me myself, I once also dived
into the depths of the ocean,
was covered over and over with mud,
but at last, failed to see the truth,
and was struggling to get back.

After following the raging current,
which disappeared in the middle of the sea,
I was happy to reach the shore,
once again wild and free.

Turn of eras

Distorted faces everywhere,
everywhere crazy ideas,
I am falling out of time
even falling out of tears.

Things are changing,
but not me with them,
and I refuse to atone for others
who are able to do so then.

I see their woes
and I see their pain,
but what I can´t change
I will avoid in future time.

Because the time has come
to protect my soul
and to keep my luck safe away
from anything cruel.

I surely won´t sacrifice it,
surely not even for you,
because you are nothing but another theft,
with whom I had to do.

Until your heart feels it

There is no sense
in telling you the words
that you have heard so often before,
there is no sense
in complimenting you,
I don´t want to set your head out of order
or to befool you.

You should not learn the meaning by words
of what I feel for you,
I would rather run straight through the desert,
just to make your heart feel
in the way I do.

If you are walking outside through the rain
and noboby is there to comfort you,
my door will always stand open here,
just to make your heart feel
in the way I do.

If you feel guilty of everything,
and your street sticks in the mud,
I will build up a new one for you,
just to make your heart feel
in the way I do.

I know
we are strangers to each other
and by now, your love doesn´t belong to me,
but it showed me the way to you,
just to make your heart feel in the way I do.

And until you can finally sense it
and the decision can be made up by you,
it really doesn´t matter to me
if I make a fool of myself for thee.

Till such time as my feelings
have finally touched your soul,
no one can ever lead me astray,
or drive me away from my goal.

Dance on the waves

My fortune is dancing on the water
and keeps smiling at me,
finally it asks me in deepest earnest,
if we could jump together right into the sea.

I shrug my shoulders,
because I don´t know
and I answer:
„I never ever tried it out
and maybe I´ll drown with you.“

But it bolsters me up and waves at me:
„Don´t worry about that at all,
I promise you, you soon will wonder
how good this lastly can be!“

So I dive into the water
and the waves are carrying me away,
my fortune and me float to a far off place
and I wish I was there to stay.

How could I ever stand still at the shore
all these long years ago,
regarding the others yearningly
how with the waves they flow.

Departure

Thunder over the mountains,
lightnings on the sea,
I pack my bags very swiftly
and get ready to go.

The air seems to be loaded,
and I´m like electrified,
I am running through the streets confused,
not knowing if I am to live or to die.

Everybody is on their departure,
and finally I am, too,
a new sound of life
is vibrating from my belly
right down to my toe.

I just start running off quickly
before I can see any aim,
I simply hope that by running
new ways come up for me again.

Come along with me,
if you dare,
and I swear you soon will see,
life is always changing its colours
if you yourself turn thee.

Self-deception

You have always been the one
who is stronger than me,
and it will only take a short time
until you wish to be free.

Let the door finally shut
and deny yourself the very last glance,
here is neither a place to look back,
nor a chance to arrange something in advance.

You will be free
and so will I,
moment so much-longed for,
there is nothing that keeps me here any longer,
apart from a promise
that burns my soul.

But I know for sure
that I deceive myself,
because what´s gone won´t come again.
Even a promise can´t rescue love,
and who´s the first to walk off
doesn´t matter then.

I´ll be with you

We all stagger through our lives
without looking on either sides,
happy to have found a way
that we think will always guide.

We are unable to realize
that a lot of people are like us,
and are astonished about a tear
rising in the other one´s eyes thus.

Like ships in a storm we are bound to waver
from time to time and from place to place.
And at the end, we don´t know much more
and are doomed to die at last.

Mostly, we can only manage
to live our everyday life.
We are prisoners of the present,
unable to shape life´s future side.

But I swear I will be with you
when your sun is setting down,
when the shadows of the night
fall on your shoulders
and make your face frown.

When you head off
for your final journey,
and it´s time for a last good-by,
I promise I will embrace your life softly
until it slips away for to die.

Bound to forget

Bound to oblivion are our souls
regardless of whether we like it or not
and in the fight for our remembrance,
the light of memory is finally shot.

We try to hold on to the very something
that in no way can be held
and in the course of the years
even your face is doomed to fade.

The sound of your so wildly loved voice
falls out of my ears bit by bit
and all these painfully suffered nights
occur to me strange, I must admit.

A door has lastly closed for good
and won´t ever be opened again,
and suppressed by the shadows of oblivion
our love will be extinguished in the end.

Journey into the past

Come on, let us ride the steam engine,
by that already your mother once went.
We enter the train here in Hamburg
and carry on until its Danish end.

Come on, let us have a trip
to the far off yesterdays,
the whistling of the engine will soon resound,
and I like to listen to what it says.

Behind every house,
there is a little sheepfold
and the animals live close to men.
Everyone knows how to repair the dikes
and to make them give shelter from the sea again.

A house is not built here on one´s own,
that would offend common decency,
the whole village has to come around
to finally get the work done.

People´s skin is brown and weather-beaten,
it seems to like the rain and the storm,
no one remembers how it originally looked like,
this time is too long gone.

Take a few steps backwards with me
and enter this time machine at last,
the whistling of the engine is not far away
and will come to your ears fast.

The days are full of heavy work
from the dawn until the dusk
and the earth sticks to the farmers´ fingers
like to the iron the rust.

Nature evokes superstition
that heavily lays on the minds
and sometimes you have to be a psychic
to sidestep the danger
that somewhere hides.

Come on, let us have a trip
to the far off yesterdays,
the whistling of the engine will soon resound,
and I like to listen to what it says.

Even eight children in one household
are not rarely to be found,
because the farms have to be kept on running
and to relax is on nobody´s mind.

Lethal diseases come and go
and medicine is hardly to get,
doctors are far off and too expensive,
it´s cheaper to die in one´s bed.

Come on, enter this train at last,
because it now won´t wait too long,
take a look at your ancestors lives
and listen to their song.

Full moon and empty heart

Full moon and empty heart,
your cold beauty reminds me
of long gone hurt.

Of someone standing
at the window now,
because the magic of its rays
has turned his head somehow.

As he did it with me
and a thousand others
as his great success began.
And in an ill kind
the pain does me good
that forces him to run.

Nevertheless, I can hardly escape
from the magic in this night
of a full moon,
from the certainty
that we both admire this planet,
lighting in such a soft tone.

The fool

I must have been a fool
to want you,
the one who is loved by everybody,
and who uses others only
for a kind of funny love study.

I must have been a fool
to have left you again and again
only to find out
living without you is impossible
and to start the same.

Only to crawl back to you
like an animal on all fours,
begging you to stay forever
and to call me yours.

Long since I know
it´s wrong what I´m doing,
long since it´s time
to choose another way of living.

But what is the meaning of right
and what is that of wrong?
As long as my heart is tied up to you
I can´t choose another way
because it isn´t over
until it is gone.

And I will stay a fool
for all this time
until at last your star
will no longer shine.

Autumn storms

Autumn storms drive colored leaves
all the way around me,
arouse pretty pictures
that I´ve nearly forgotten
and always refused to see.

Your tender glance,
your loving hand,
your stormy embrace
in the summer sand.

Now it seems to be
such a long time ago
that you ran away from me,
and since such a long time
every day is winter,
the summer vanished with thee.

My days are now
long and lonesome,
and my ears are deaf
to spring time´s song,
even the pain doesn´t survive
the long winter´s night,
and each little morning´s hope
will immediately be gone.

Summers are passing by quietly,
they don´t mean anything to me,
and in the sole time,
that I can feel something
red and gold leaves are tumbling
down from the garden´s tree.

The near winter reminds me
of what I have lost
forevermore,
the night has seized hold of me,
and locked the bright day´s door.

Stay with me

So often I have maltreated my feet
with long and painful marches,
so often I have toppled over them,
looking in vain for shelter in some arches.

Have sinned and laughed at others,
have walked on without any concern,
repeated mistakes again and again
and it made no difference to me
to see them return.

Have staggered from the right to the left,
no firm foothold in sight,
until destiny once again
threw me back on your side.

Now I´m standing here,
astonished to find out
that all ways led to thee.
And hadn´t there been
your helping hand,
I surely still wouldn´t be free.

So what does remain to be hoped for?
What do I wish from you?
Stay with me,
don´t turn away,
stay with me,
even if it was only
for the next day.

Melancholy

Like the first dew on the first blossom
in the early morning sun,
it lays down on me during my day,
mantling my face in the night´s run.

It can be so soft and tender,
but rules me with an iron fist,
slows down every flight to its end
no matter how fair it is.

Melancholy
will haunt me forever,
wherever I´ll put my feet down,
it will always be on my heels
and forces my face to frown.

I dive into the depth of the night
in search of an honest kiss,
looking for
a truthful embrace,
for somebody saying
It´s you that I miss.

But even love
won´t bring relief to me,
if I try to enforce it this way,
and finally I stand in front of my door,
embracing my own emptiness
that had never faded away.

And if at one time
life puts its arms around me
and my fortune is so close by,
melancholy is still a part of me,
and I know deep inside
it will never go away.

Time of clouds

Hardly when I´ve seen the stuff
that has to be done at work,
I feel reluctance in my heart,
and I have to kill a piece of me
in order to be able to start.

Always the same troubles and duties,
all the same day after day,
and I´m wondering
when it will have finally killed me
and thereafter blown away.

But like all the others,
I need the money to survive,
we are all nailed on the eternal wheel,
far away from what really counts in life.

Sometimes I furtively look through the window
to the clouds swaying high above me,
they are happily dancing in heaven,
so lighthearted and so admirably free.

And my heart tenses up
each time I see them swaying so free,
and once again I realize
there must be more in this life to see.

A different life,
man, what a dream!
Reality blurs before my eyes
and I fly out of this room.

I simply don´t like to return,
not today and not tomorrow,
not back to this life of daily routine,
not back to my daily horror.

If it already came to the point
that a cloud would sway down to me,
it would surely take me up to the sky
and shatter my eternal wheel.

Poems about Bob Dylan

Warm colours

Warm colours softly shimmer
through the walls of your face,
shining like a morning´s rainbow,
spreading all its grace.

Sheltered behind sarcasm and irony,
there lies your very true sight,
deeply buried in the darkness,
far off any light.

But the years digged rifts
in your facade of stone,
they no longer can be patched,
your true self is coming along.

Let the magic of your colours
finally see the light of the day,
I know you can overcome the hurtings
and make the colours here to stay.

Going, going, gone

Going, going, gone,
you firstly thought these words,
dreaming of a different life to begin.

Like you I now feel the temptation
to give up everything again,
to tear the old into pieces
in order to start anew then.

So often I have already set off,
but never did I arrive,
so often I thought
the luck rests with me,
while it was already on the road,
heading to be free.

Maybe it wants to be with those
who manage to keep calm,
who have the power
to let things slide
and not always look
for something new to come along.

For Bob Dylan

In the darkest hour of my nights,
in all my despair and deepest sorrow,
only your raucous voice is left
that robs the demons their tomorrow.

You are the one,
who had so often been driven down to his knees,
who knows all about the abyss of despair
and how to survive the blues.

And if your songs wouldn´t exist,
would I be able to see a new morning?
They take away the burden from my shoulder,
ease my sorrow and chase it with forceful warning.

What you have done for my heart,
I will never forget for the sake of heaven,
soul whisperer of my endless nights,
verse magician Bob Dylan.

The old songwriter

And once again
you stand there alone,
all alone with your harmonica,
your piano is no longer there
and your hands refuse
to play the guitar.

But there is still
the same old fire burning,
still shining with the same old force,
which will soon take away my breath
and inflames the magic once more.

And your spell will never fade
as long as you sing one note,
as long as death,
after long struggle,
will take away your breath.

The return

Born in a foreign country,
so far away from home,
with strange parents who didn´t understand,
you always felt so alone.

You had to start the odyssey
back to yourself then,
the pain drove you down
the streets of yearning,
looking for the destination of man.

And each experience brought you closer,
each scar a step to your aim,
no matter, if success or failure,
both were part of the game.

A storm was raging wild and free
in your restless soul,
taking you to places, people, and things
which otherwise
would have never been your goal.

Slowly, but unstoppable,
your ship now comes into port,
finally willing to grant you peace
as lifelong struggle´s reward.

After all these years on the road,
you lastly seem to arrive,
after all these battles
you won back yourself,
finding your homeland
and dancing the last jive.

The change

Once again you have pulled off the feat
and reinvented yourself,
finding the key to another being
and using it on your behalf.

And all the old melodies
finally obtain a new sense,
while history had yet
coated them with dust,
they were already dying along,
covered with lots of rust.

But you have awaked them
from a deep slumber,
have finally kissed them alert,
and suddenly I did realise
how much they´ve been missed by my heart.

Sweet by sweet

Sweet by sweet
and side by side
your words fly through the air,
bringing healing to my wounded soul
from whatever hurtings
that were there.

Note by note
and letter by letter
you create a land of the new-born,
far away from all these blind people
whose souls are hopeless and forlorn.

Bit by bit
and step by step
I feel the power rising in me,
until I finally leave this cramped valley
up to the highway of the free.

Walking through the fire

I see you walking through the fire,
and I wonder how you survive,
when I touched only one single hot spot,
it endangered my whole life.

I feel the words inside of me
pleading to become alive,
but I know I can´t stand the pressure,
if they are all well-known outside.

So I let them flow down on the paper,
but don´t take much effort in popularizing,
I give in to the coward in me,
thus being sure of surviving.

The book of life

Life once lent you a magic pen
to write up all of your thoughts,
all of your feelings and all of your fears,
with which you have ever fought.

And as lastly the days became dimmer
and your eyes could hardly see,
it still brought the pen for you
and lit a candle for thee.

So page after page was turned over,
running to a huge number,
and to see you now still working thus
for me is the greatest wonder.

And when someday life will decide
that your work has finally been done,
it will hand us over this book as a present
of one of its greatest sons.

For more texts see:

www.gudrunheller.wix.com/autorin